Tapestry Of My Heart

A Collection of Poems on Emotions

Suvarna Sonavane

BookLeaf
Publishing

India | USA | UK

Made with ❤ on the BookLeaf Publishing Platform

www.bookleafpub.in

www.bookleafpub.com

Dedication

To the all emotions and feelings that evolved, us to shape up as a Human. To them who loves to explore the mind and behaviour of human psychology that contains various nature of human-emotions that are essence of life, that make us.

Preface

"**Tapestry of my Heart:** *A Collection of Poems on Emotions*" was born out of the complex and interwoven person's innermost feelings, memories, emotions, relationships and experiences of life that shape-up all the Humankind.

These poems symbolizes the intricate fabric of one's heart, where every thread epitomizes a significant moment or connection in their life; much like a Tapestry, that is made-up of many different parts that come together to create a whole-picture.

The collection of these poems are like a Tapestry with various colours and patterns, you will experience all multifaceted nature of human emotions, including Joy, Sorrow, Love, Friendship, Desire and everything in between.

Acknowledgements

Special Thanks to all my readers, whose love for Poetry and for indulging to know human nature, this helps to mend us as a complete human that is considerate and thoughtful to show WHO WE ARE. Thanks to the people around me who kept me motivating to write and for being with me in this new journey of writing. Your support and appreciation are deeply valued.

Poem 1

You and I ...

You and I like a pair of Moon and Star in the sky.
You and I like Earth and Sky meets at the Horizon Line.

Knowing they will meet never,
Still they don't Despair ever.

We have seen a phase, when our clan flutter
Doubting how long we will stay Together.
Eventually, they started staking
It will stay Long and Forever.

Love is not simply being Together,
It's an Everlasting feeling that builds
The Bond stay more merrier than Ever.

Poem 2

HOPE

Performing the Routine stuff can make
You feel bored and alone.
Don't worry, being alone ain't bad at all.

It's an honour to take some hold of you.
Stay calm even if everything is falling apart.

As I will always be there to light up the Dark.

Poem 3

RACE OF MANKIND

In the Race of Mankind.
Everyone is looking for Fake Space to just unwind.

Trying to Seize the Spirit of life by
Thinking to Raise the Hope of Sigh.

Unknowingly connecting and hunting
The friendship and support.
Failing to misunderstand it as Love and
Just pointing the relationship as Discord.

Everyone forgets the beauty of every relationship.
Is being in Debt of gravity and the Accord.

Poem 4

SOMEONE

Have you ever met Someone Special?
And fall for him or her Right there.

Even though you both are Strangers!
Still you feel like you have loved Rangers.
Get your courage, as words will be lost
Racing your heartbeat faster.

If Love needs merit, nothing overcast the sharing soul.
Yes, Friendship and Love is full of Emotions.
There's no Logic, it's passion with Magical Moments.

Poem 5

YOUR WORDS

True Buddy it's your words that makes me –

Feel Beautiful keeping away from flaws.
Feel Stronger swaying away all fragility.
Feel Special striking off the usual things.
Feel Jovial and Cheerful whisking all the
Gloomy clouds hovering around.

Yes, you are my Best Buddy! And
Only you can put me on, it's the only song
I would Love to sing all along.

Poem 6

TIME

Be the Light in the darkness that
Spreads the sparkling shower of
Stars on the Horizon.

Be the Smile that dissipates away
The sadness just like the
Scintillating Sun spreads its veil of Bliss.

The feeling of half the world is deep in sleep
And there are two individuals
Sharing their Minds.

Like Time stays still when we
Depart and suddenly you're like
Wow Time has flown being in your arms.

Poem 7

SOMEWHERE...

Let's go somewhere
Far and Peaceful
To the Meadows
Sit down and watch Sunset
About sitting and enjoying the
Good Vibes

Beautiful indeed
Such views are treasures.
Just sitting, absorbing the vibes
Watching the Sunset and Night Rise.

Poem 8

WHO IS SHE?

I cried aloud and settled to feel the soft tender
Touch of unwavering Love.
I tried to open my eyes and saw an enchanted gaze,
Looking at me affectionately.
I wondered who is SHE?

I saw her sleepless nights and
Lovely lullaby songs for me.
She helped me to take my steps one at a time.
Every time it was one-step closer to my Dreams.
I wondered who is SHE?

She stood like a Rock, supporting and encouraging me.
Always patting my back to do more,
So I could Soar High.
I wondered who is SHE?

Stepping in my adulthood finally, I understood –
She is irreplaceable. Nothing can be
So Pure and Pristine like
The Unsullied Love of MOTHER.

I dressed up my wedding clothes and
Was ready for the Vows and Cries.
I wanted to take a final look at myself,
So I looked in the Mirror and
I wondered who is SHE?

A tight warm hug from behind leaning on my shoulder,
She whispered softly – Dear, that's no one else but
"YOU"

It's an ongoing Journey and Time-Travel.
Perhaps one day I'll know who SHE is.

Poem 9

YOU ARE MY SEASHORE

Smelling the Freedom of Embracing You.
Watching you so Close and Deep as if
Eyes penetrating through your heart with every
Rhythm of your Heartbeat.

Leaning of your shoulder as if Amber
Dazzled on the Horizon.
Tousling your hair with fingers like
Stroking down the Landscape on the
Canvas as if settling Sun is the Masterpiece.

Yes it's your Love that feels like Honeyed
Rays spreading across the waves makes
me feel Refreshed and Tranquil.

Savouring every moment being with you
FOREVER and EVER.

Poem 10

LIFETIME

My heart says write something special for him!
What can I think of coz your kindness makes me go
Speechless and somehow I keep losing my words.

Yet I will say our bonding is so Beautiful and Strong.
Something so perfect you will never want to miss.
Like this Beautiful Sunset,
It's revealing a gorgeous blend of
Scarlet and Yellow; painting the Sky
So high making it breath-taking sight...

So do we match up as we are true Twin-flames that
Claim to be Together and Ever for a LIFETIME.

Poem 11

DEAR FRIEND

Happy to have friend like you.
Who is ready to lift me whenever I feel blue...

Making me smile with the smallest things you do
Swaying away all the gloomy effects.
Just wondering how you manage to do.

Your friendship means a lot.
I wish to have you for forever.

Will you too be feeling the same as I do?

Poem 12

CRESCENT MOON

With you, every moment feels like Magic.
Nothing can be as Pure as LOVE.

Everything is so
Calm and Serene
Yet the eagerness
Of meeting each
Other feels the
Warmth in the air.

Be mine Crescent MOON -
That evokes beauty of night
Appearing daily and not the
Halley's Comet...
It comes once in a Blue Moon
My Love

Poem 13

HEARTBREAK

Shattered and Devasted were all my thoughts of her.
Somehow, I figured out to wrap up
My Melancholy heart for sure.

I thought it was the end of my true Love of course,
It was not fictional nor from the extra-terrestrial world.

All things went topsy-turvy
Shaking all moments and memories crushed with tears.
I didn't leave any stone unturned of
Thoughts and feeling for her with losing fear.

Nothing could help me correct the messed up life
As if missing a piece of jigsaw puzzle.
You were a key part of my complete depiction of US.

Albeit, you thought I would be in grief
With deep scars never to stay in the bliss forever.

Time is the best medicine that
Healed me to regain myself.
Giving me a lesson to Rise again with Vigour.
A chance to view that there is so much more
That needs my Love and Attention Ever.

It's only a HEARTBREAK and not the end of my life.
I learnt a lesson to be Happy and Jovial
For the love of near ones Sake.

Poem 14

TOUCH

Your touch ignites the charge and
Takes in the wildfire arm.
Drizzle starts and flow just the way you kissed me first.

I missed you around!
You want to know how much My Love
The fragrance of your intriguing body
Still skips my Heartbeat more

Will the urge of your warmth
Can quench the thirst of my Love?
For YOU are me and I'm within you for Sure.

Poem 15

ETERNAL

The warmth of your breath hits my skin,
A gentle caress marked so clean.
With every whisper our Love awakens and unfolds,
In the most Magical & Tender way of getting your hold.

In silence, our hearts beat as One.
A Love so strong it has just begun.
A beautiful melody our Love ignites
With every passing night.

Our hearts beating faster,
Our breaths growing harder still.
Both lost & engrossed in this blissful thrill.
Beneath the starry night sky,
These moments will survive.
Starting each new day until the ETERNAL arrives.

Poem 16

DANDELION FIELDS

Dreamt of being with you under the cherry blossom
With Dandelions around,
some in Red and White
And some in Blue.
I wish to be Dandelion for their Parachute-like structure
Soothes my mind with the act of Dissilient.
Their thriving nature in a challenging state
Shows the kind of Resilient.

Watching Meadows and tall grass,
With Sun high up in the sky
Holding your hands and
Talking endlessly sitting with you
As no one is around us for Miles and Miles.
In the Twilight strong wind gushing quiet
Except for birds, chirping as there is still
Brightness in the sky.

Being in your arms, we can feel all the
Dandelions touching our feet.
Strands of your hair on my face and
Tousling on your cheek.
If you could see through my Kaleidoscope, you will find
Whispering trees, Painted skies, and Velvety land
Covered in Dewdrops with cool breeze around.

Labyrinth of my mind had something so Surreal in the
Realms of my Dreams.

Poem 17

BEAUTY AND THE BEAST

Bella's golden hue long hair locks
Are glittering and flowing along.
With the wind trying to catch hold of the Prince's heart.

She is looking Angelic just like Exotic Rose.
The fire of her soul is reflecting deeply
In her eyes so close.
Surely, they can try to captivate and
Steal Prince Heart today.

Bella is beautiful and the Prince was a Daemon.
Yet! Bella came along to submit her.
The Prince is not in a mode of acceptance.

Bella was afraid what if the love is not there.
Still her acts gave the love of her life and life for love.
Whatsoever, at the end Beauty loved the Beast.

Poem 18

DEAR DIARY

Dear Diary you always helped me
To ink down my thoughts
With my beautiful blue feather pen, I adore.
The moment I open you, the pages start
To smell like Petrichor.
I named her Aegis as my world revolves around her!

All my Dreams are longing to get her hold.
In addition, my eyes couldn't get it's uphold.
She is my Secret-Keeper that inscribes all the facts.
My Love for her is an Immutable act.

If you look, you will know that Diary is not just a book.
It's the protector of my feelings and emotions
Poured out of my heart.
She has cherished all my Dreams and Goals;
Vicissitudes of life.

A loyal friend I am able to find, it will sound good
If I say, it's a reflection of my Soul.

Covered beautifully with metallic edges
To keep away from Evil's Eye.
Writing with my blue feather Pen seems
Like holding a Magical Wand,
It helps to weave my thoughts with
Little Confidante that is set on my desk.

Poem 19

LOVE LETTER

Oh my Chivalrous Prince
I know this letter will sprinkle the Ethereal Glow
On your gracious and enchanting aspects.

Meeting you is one of the best things
That has happened in my life.
I have finally discovered someone truly special.
All my Mornings start and Day ends with your thoughts.
I hope you will stay with me Forever!

You are the most Charming and Gallant person I know.
You are Unique and Unforgettable;
I love and cherish you with my Heart.
You make me Smile as if no one else can.
You know me better than anyone would ever know me.

Being in your amorous hug
Is the most amazing feeling in the world.

Albeit, you are far I can feel you so close.
Hoping you think of me and wonder where will I be.
I would love if our paths converge so I could
Cherish those moments for sure.
Holding my breath;
Until a Serendipitous encounter unfolds.

Poem 20

COLOURS OF LIFE

I have a vintage cuboid named "Rainbow Dash"
Withholding inside the caskets full of colours
Known as "Wonderbolts".

I picked up a chest of Scarlet Red – only to find
The "Love" that wants to acquire the "Passion" to flex
About its "Aggression" filled with Dominance.
My Hazel gaze caught hold of Emerald Green
That wants to Rebirth from the ashes of hope
And turn away all the futility.

Nothing can be as irresistible
As the Ebony Night Sky Black
That overcast every shade you have
With Power to hold up high.
Flamboyant flamingo in Roseate Pink tenders
Every heart that everyone seeks to Love Ebulliently.

Sometimes Truth is conspicuous as pure as Crystal
Similar to Alabaster White.
Sometimes it can be Leaden Grey doubting the
Veracity of the story as it feels Sombre and Gloomy.

Oh! My Electric Blue will always be fun
Creating a Hope on the Horizon.
You will admire my candour if I tell
That my melodious Canary
Impresses with its full of Yellow Plumage.

A Symphony of colours in a mystic maze
Amethyst Purple gives a touch of Ethereal Beauty
With Luxury and Style.
In a Realm of Serenity, it evokes Regal Mystery.

Envisage a life full of Colours that
Behold the Beauty with Spice.

Poem 21

MEMORIES

Basking in the Sunshine in a leisurely way
Sun casting its magical Ombre tinted veil
Around honeyed rays of Gold.

The Ocean stretched out, splashing the waves
Every drop full of Memories to be
Reminiscent of Memories
Azure blue that merged with the
Sky on the distant horizon.
Secluding myself from the present and future,
I read about Teleports in most of Fantasy books,
Can we have it in reality and
We transport with just a little shook.

A fog lifting, revealing cherished memories
Taking a trip down memory lane,
I wish to live those moments again!
Yet, I could only managed to freeze them in time.

Clicking the miniscule moments
In each-and-every frame.

The picture album treasured with me
Like a Golden Compass.
That shows the way to the Attic of my past.
My mind contents all memories with
Segments of emotions like
Tapestry made up of Joy and Laughter, Tears and Fears.
As if Knots in a string of beads.